POETRY
Power of the Mind

Mother Sarasvati: Goddess of knowledge

BLOSSOM LIKE A LOTOUS

BY KARRAN P. DEOKARRAN

Nalenine Pillia Deokarran & Karran P. Deokarran

The Author

My fellow Brothers and Sisters I greet you in the name of God

The very thought of putting these poems into a book is beyond My controlled it was by the will of God that these inspiration blossom like a lotus from within the self. I always hope and pray that I will someday be able to say some good things to mankind, I only hope and pray that whoever read these lines would not look at the words but search deep within thyself for the hidden nectar. The world before us is only a stepping stone to the real world Where all the beauty awaits every one, so why waste our time here We must continue our journey, the road will be rough but with our good deeds We will be given help on our way, the corrupt practice of man today have sprang Out of lust and passion for material wealth which we all die and leave The lines in these poems are design for the ordinary man who might not have a degree or masters But who has the ability to use his or her common sense to understand things The knowledge might be of a high quality the purpose is not to memories the different lines And then sing them to others my intention is to let these knowledge become wisdom, whoever Read them with a little practice can make the world a better place to live, I came from a poor humble but highly religious family with a Hindu background but I always support every other religion My father always says every religion teaches truth love and honesty and if every reader could have Practice these three words how great this world would have been, I wish to dedicate this book to my wife Nalenine Pillai Deokarran who have always support me in good times and in bad times she is a symbol of what a wife should be she give me strength and courage to stand the many trials and temptation. To my Four children Latchmi ,Menakshi ,Bhanmatie and Chuniram and my three grandson Aryan , Davin and Chitanand, my three son- in- law, Satash Deonarine, Parsaram Persaud, Steve choitall, if you want to treasure anything from your father Grandfather and father- in- law, then you must continue his path of helping every living creature while you traverse this lone journey to eternity , to all my friends and family the only gift I have for you is to choose any Line from any poem practice them and let it be my gift to you, finally I wish to express my heartfelt Thanks to all the struggling Guyanese Brothers and Sisters who want to see a bright future for their Country, A special thanks to Mr. James McMinnon from long island U.S.A. A good friend who I meet on my job place his lineage is Irish very Religious and helpful, I also want to extend a special thanks to a brilliant spiritual teacher who I meet in New York a Guyanese by birth living in the U,S.A he is Pandit Mahendranauth Doobay Pandit Doobay have become a close friend and a loyal teacher to me ,I also want to say a special thank you to Pandit Krishanand Sahadeo and his son Darsahand Persaud who hail from my neighboring community in Guyana and live in the U.S.A. they always keep encouraging me to keep writing their advice was of great help to me, I also wishes to thank the following persons Pt. Krishna, and his brother Puran from Krishna Bazar,Alma Singh a Guyanese living in New York, and Keane lazemo a Trinidadian live in Florida

KARRAN P. DEOKARRAN J.P.

A MESSAGE

The time has come when the wise men of the world will have to put their earning into real investment, the intelligent sector have done their investment which have brought huge profit of corruption discrimination, war , displacement, hunger, and a high percent of immoral behavior among mankind, this investment will lead the world to its final destruction, which is already in its making I feel the time has come for the few wise men that has been walking the earth who do not carry any burden on their shoulder such as a degree, masters or diploma but carry simplicity, love , honesty, sincerity and truth , ,they cannot be found in Temple ,Church or Mosque, they cannot be found in Government structure ,they walk the road begging mankind to do a little good for the world while they search their heart for answers oh man when you such person come before you consider yourself fortunate, give them your love and admiration wish them well they are the savior of the world.

KARRAN.P. DEOKARRAN

BIOGRAPHY

Born on the 31st March 1958 in a little village call bath Mahaicony in Guyana south America to the parents of Deokarran and Koomarie both my mom and dad had previous marriage my dad had a son name Lakeram and my mom had a daughter name Leela my mom and Dad together had four sons and two daughters I was the eldest of six my name was given as Karran according to the Hindu book followed by Dirjodhan, Mangal, Lalchand Nandinee and Hemwantie our parents were very poor and fishing was the only means of lively hood ,I being the eldest had little chance of going to school , at the age of twelve ,I had to go with my father to catch fish and shrimp from mid night to next day ten am then from twelve I will go to school at 4th standard I had to leave school my dad will always say son never give up knowledge don't come from anywhere it is within seek god help and you will have the best of knowledge The unfolding story of my journey begin it was January 1970 at the age of twelve I started the fishing career early February my father ask me to plant the Holika plant (a Castrol plant) which will be burnt on the full moon night forty days from the day of the planting which will be followed by the celebration of Phagwa marking the beginning of the Hindu new year, the whole process involve fasting, feeding the plant every morning apiece of dried leaf and water Holika represent the wicked sister of an evil King who wanted to kill his son because he preach the name of God this was the beginning of my vegetarian life Holi is the destruction of evil and the protection of good this is how my father had wanted me to be on this sacred journey in this birth ,my father teach me one word (Help) he said practice this and everything else you will get , after the separation of my mother and father in 1976 my mom migrate to Suriname my Brothers and Sisters went with her I remain with my father we abandon fishing I started to work in a rice mill doing laborer work, the same year 1976 I join the P.Y.O. the youth arm of the P.P.P. this was the beginning of my political mission and so I have choose two path to carry out my mission to help mankind, Politic to help economic development and Religion for Spiritual development as I traverse this rough journey many things have happen my duty was to move ahead, in 1980 I married to Nalenine against the wishes of both side parents however it was approved by destiny because she was destine to help me in my journey she give birth to four, beautiful children namely Latchmi ,Menakshi,Bhanmatie and Chuniram. The first real trial begin when I was kidnap on the 26 of April 1989 from my home and taken to some unknown place ,it was menakshi first birthday two years later I would see her again, for six days I was kept in hiding been tortured without food and water place in a cell naked lying on a concrete floor that is always wet I was taken out on a regular, blind folded and taken to some room I will be place on a chair then I would strap everything seems to be operating electrical then I will be shock with current the voltage constantly increase then something would place over my head and will adjust squeeze my head until I lost consciousness I will beaten on my back and chest ,I will be hang by my foot in the air, then my head will be place in a toilet bowl and ice water flush on my head I would be question about the P.P.P. leaders planning to overthrow the Government I have already give up living and so I have no concern answering any question after six days I was taken to some unknown place pickup by another group taken to the police head quarter and later charge for treason taken to court and then to prison where I would spend 544days before I won my case and was release to be unite with my family again , some of the lawyers which play a very important role are Khemraj Ramjattan,Charls Ramson, Bernard DE Santos, Ralph Ramkarran, Moses Bhagwan, Amnesty international ,and a few others lawyer whose name I cannot remember, the many Guyanese living abroad and protest at the U.N. headquarter in the U.S.A. all of whom I wish to thank for their support and the courage they give during the trial. After I was release I continue political work with the P.P.P. many question was asked and is still asking why the P.P.P. play a low profile in the treason case and continue to do the same those question will be answer some time in the near future. I was one never like by many of the leading people in freedom house but was always close to Cheddi Jagan the leader one of the party the reason was I always have a different interpretation of communism I always believe the Russian and Cuban were not communist but dictator and the opportunity for individual to move up was the most difficult task, I always believed that communism can be best describe by the Holy Ramayana and the rule of king Dasarath the father of lord Rama and which is difficult to practice in this sinful age especially when truth, love, and honesty is lost the present communist system is design to help empower family and friend through a political system, on the other side the capitalist system allowed for exploitation of man by man this system will disappear over a period of time by then the world will be in poverty and both system will disappear ,let examine the system not by name but by action those who say they are communist empowering minority to control majority on the other hand those who practice capitalist system allowed minority to controlled wealth and majority to live in poverty the two system will clash one day like thunder and lighting and will vanish forever then a new system will born, a system where those empower to manage and those bless to secure wealth will work together to help the world of human live happily that system will be called humanism. This my political belief the prison life is one of fate in yourself and the courage to stand the many trials and temptation it helps me to awaken the inner self to controlled the mind and to search for answers, after I was out of prison wining my case I continue with the P.P.P. I always criticize the party system after the win in 1992 and the party become the government the government decided to hold local government election which was a bold step toward the right direction I contest the wood land/farm N.D.C. on the P.P.P. ticket and we won 10 seat and the P.N.C. 8 seat I was elected the chairman my immediate task was to win the trust and confident of the opposition this was important if we are going to help people leaders of the P.P.P. we're not happy with me and many label me as P.N.C. however, my mission was to build a great N.D.C. the job was a voluntary, it was meant to give service to the people I spent twelve years at the helm of the N.D.C. and I enjoyed every single day helping people for Cheddi Jagan he always complements me for what I am doing but the rest hate me in the party executive in 2006 the P.P.P. won the election and Bharat Jagdeo was the President he had wanted me to become the region five chairman however the party executive did not like it and we settle for the vice chairman the chairman was given a third term of failure President Jagdeo have always proven that the system was wrong but he was helpless he was made a president by those who hold the power in the party and were always deem(we put you there do what we want) lives was miserable for him I had close contact with him many time he voice his concern he want to resign but I will encourage him to stay on being the vice chairman of region five I was assign chairman of the works committee it is a powerful committee in the region it an area where corruption can be protected or can be remove there were fear everywhere because everyone know I will put a stop to many of the wrong thing happening in the region my first day in office as I sit on my chair I pull a draw from the desk there I discover an envelope with a set of transport these transport belongs to persons who had applied for house lot from the Government and the transport were to be given to the applicant, and were never to be in the vice chairman office but all the names were people living abroad the rest is a long story I took the transport to the chairman office and give him he look at me and did not say a word I then change the works committee rules from the chairman of the committee making the decision to the committee making the decision and those decision approve at the region meeting that meeting is made up of Government and opposition members so fair play was put in place contractor were been paid promptly I don't keep any one document they are sent for payment immediately this is how I streamline all the area I was in charge, health was another area I had to change a number of things to get it working in 2010 there were two contractor with two roads of nine million dollars contractor each when the works was about 15% a certain minister want me to sign payment for 90% work I refuse I was threaten by the contractor but that did not turn me I was offer two million I refuse then I wrote the incidence at the back of the voucher and leave it on my desk before leaving the office on the 24th December 2010 for a two month vacation in the united states of

America no one know I was leaving for America and that I had a permanent visa I leave Guyana on the 26 December 2010 as I step on the plane step I look at Guyana with tears in my eyes and folded hands I silently wish my country a better future because my return would be long I wrote my resignation and leave it with eldest daughter who did not manage to get her visa, corruption was the main reason for me to decide to leave Guyana my commitment to Guyana and its people are deep down in my heart my life was at stakes when minister want me to get into corruption who will protect me in the fight against corruption Although I am living in America my mind always with the Guyanese , because of this love I begin a spiritual search to find an answer to the real problem in Guyana which I wrote in a few beautiful verses title (50 years of pain and struggle) it is the answer to Guyana problem a final sacrifice I am prepared to make, No Government can settle in Guyana peaceful the slaves and indenture labor came with spiritual power no one ever show respect for their soul and spirit we have to understand that as human beings we are not this body which is made up of five element we are souls and spirits with great powers and can do great things even when we leave this body unless certain act are carried out for the soul and spirit by those who remain in the human body priority for those action begin with the close relative these action is important for the continuation of the human existence .it doesn't matter how educated, how smart or how honest one is as soon he or she get into public office a spiritual force is there to take care of you , such power will always miss lead you unless you can satisfy its need if one should take a careful look at the things happening at the mandir (KALI) if one take a careful look at the behavior of the pujari or priest and his follower one can understand the power of the spirit pretending to be holy giving themselves name of holy people unless one can live a holy life how can the incarnation of god speak through these people who do not live a righteous life all of this had happen because we were not living a righteous life these spirit take controlled of our body and do all crazy things I go through many trials and am saying what I have experience in this life to learn the secret I had to get involve here is where country and people have find themselves in problem any one can sit in one of these mandir just pay careful attention to the language of the pujari when the spirit would speak through them you will quickly understand what is happening in this world to combat such situation it takes one to undertake great sacrifice honesty in everything love for the world truth the watch word believe in God every religion must be seen as a part of the almighty we must able to remove from our heart distrust ,hatred, lust ,greed and egoism pay respect for our fore parents who made great sacrifice who work as slave and indenture labor for the good of their off spring I urge every Guyanese to pay tribute to our fore parent crime and corruption will over and a great nation will take birth in this world ,I always believe that every nation have the right to determine their own path of development my reason is every nation have their own culture, some have their own language their natural resource will be different and so their development strategy will be different there is only one nation on earth which have all the natural resource the whole world might have and don't have a development strategy after fifty years of independence is the country of my birth Guyana in south America, a country of millions of acre of land and it citizens have a problem getting a house lot to build a house to live in or an acre of land to plant food to survive. Every government elected to office spend their first two year searching to see what the previous Government did the next two year is to find ways and means to help family and friends and to secure for themselves the last year is to prepare for the next election and how much promise would be made to win another five year term, Guyana have a population of five hundred thousand people with some of the most brilliant minds some of the most skillful farmers and yet we are the second poorest nation in the world, what a great joke in a land of the greatest political jokers ,why I came to the U.S.A. to learn what is America and why everyone coming to America what I found what the politician doing in my country Guyana the people are allowed to do it in the U.S.A. the freedom to become rich materially ,but I search to find moral value, cultural value religious value in practice have all disappear what I found growing very fast is hatred, lust, anger. Crime and corruption the long term result is destruction of man by man all I can do is to hope and pray that a few good men will remain to start a new generation after god will put an end to all the wrong on earth, my fellow Brothers and Sisters, Mothers and Fathers it is our moral obligation to preserve the human race even if it is one percent all it take is a little practice of honesty ,love be truthful to whatever you do try to help your fellow human believe that there is a god above looking at everything we do when we leave this body we take nothing with us we should protect nature ,we must not want to kill the cow for food which take care of us from a baby to old age by giving us milk to live strong and healthy this we must preserved this is the biggest sin we are committing as human I only hope and pray that my message will help in some way to change the mind of man every Poem is a message from the heart from the inner selves something I do not want to keep for myself read and cherish God blessing be with everyone no matter which religion you belong to God is one he take different form to please different nation

Karran Persaud Deokarran J.P.   (Vickram)

26 April 2016 Brooklyn New York U.S.A.

A GREAT POET 3000YRS AGO

Where there is Righteousness in the heart
There is Beauty in the Character
When there is Beauty in the character
There will be Harmony in the home
When there is harmony in the home
There will be order in the country
When there is order in the country
There will be peace in the world

By Kaniyan Pungundranar
Indian Poet

Every action that Man preform in this World begin from a place call home and by a mother and a father they are responsible for building a child future whatever moral or immoral value are instill into the child that help to formulate the world behavior in this context Kaniyan want to remind us that if we want a World of Peace it will have to start from our home, I salute Kaniyan for reminding us how we can have peace in this world

This book is dedicated to my Wife Nalenine Pillia Deokarran

Her Courage, Loyalty and Patience is my Inspiration

Contents

My prayer

My salutation to thee oh mom and dad
Thank you for bringing me into this world
Thank you for teaching me to walk the path of righteousness
And to worshipped the almighty god for happiness

My humble salutation to thee oh Supreme God
For creating and preserving this universe
Give me an opportunity to experience your creation
Give me knowledge and wisdom so I can find salvation

Give me a chance to love and served you with devotion
Give me courage and faith to stand the many trials and temptation
Bless me with the will to served others
Bless me so when I leave this body I will be with your forever

Oh supreme god allowed me to worshipped you in all thy form and glory
Shower your love and admiration upon all too live happy
Oh my god if there is anything you wish to bless me with
Let it be thy will that I never live to regret

Let from birth to birth experience your greatness
And understand your creation which can give real happiness
Give me health and strength to chant the glory of your name
Let the tears from my eyes fill your heart with love oh divine

Oh Almighty God

Bless my hands to help others
Bless my feet to walk the righteous path forever
Bless my eyes to see your creation
Bless my taught so I can achieve salvation

Bless me with knowledge and wisdom
Bless me to reach your kingdom
Bless me with courage to face all temptation
Bless me to achieve emancipation

Bless me with truth and honesty
Bless me with peace love and prosperity
Bless me with the will to offer forgiveness
Bless me with courage to remove others sadness

Bless me to bring cheers to the destitute and sick
Bless my hands to used your magic trick
Bless me to lead others to righteousness
Bless me so that whatever I do I will have success

By Karran P. Deokarran

My story

From a poor humbly family I was born
Fishing my first job for a daily bread to earn
I was only twelve years catching fish without fear
It was karma [past action] who cares

In pouring rain and the dark of the night
With water to my neck this my plight
Staying by my father side I care nothing
Only thinking of an honest living

Schooling I know I will lost forever
Every day father would say help others
Surrender yourself to the feet of the almighty
He will bless you with knowledge for eternity

From a fisherman to a laborer
Then a carpenter and then a farmer
Then a politician and to a social worker
Then to an administer and to a secret admirer

Poverty makes many demands
Everywhere I go I try to give a helping hand
Those who lust for position see me their enemy
Sacrifice for others make me happy

None will carry their wealth to their grave
Many obstacles I had to brave
From righteousness I will never part
Until from this body I depart

50 Years of Pain and Struggle

They came in chain from Africa
To slave in Beautiful Guyana
They were brought from far away India
To labored in Beautiful Guyana

Time have destroyed their identity
Their culture and tradition were lost in history
Their language was compromised by the slave master
Their Religion was sacrifice for schooling which was a
disaster

Cuffy and Damon wage a battle for freedom
The Indian selfishness were held at ransom
Jagan and Burnham continue the struggle
Unity play a great role; freedom became possible

Then came the 26 of May 1966 bright like a star
The cries of a Nation turn into joy near and far
The struggle of our fore parent were forgotten
50 years later their sacrifice become the Nation burden

As we hoist the golden Arrow head for the 50th time
No amount of speeches and promises can remove the nation
pains
Oh leaders I humbly ask that you seek the divine
intervention
Ask for forgiveness and give our fore parent an honorable
salutation

Dancing on the street is only more molestation
The fighting spirit of our ancestor need salvation
No Government will find peace in my Beautiful Guyana
Unless we join hands together to liberate our ancestor

The tears of our ancestor only brought flood each year
Their anger brought drought and fear
Their love keeps the nation existing but in poverty
This is how Guyana will be unless their souls are liberated
by the Almighty

Oh my dear Guyana my salutation to thee
The sweat and blood of your children Brought freedom to
thee
What have we achieved 50 years later
Corruption, hatred, lust, crime and anger.

Karran P. Deokarran (Vickram) J.P.

Dedicated to Guyana 50th independence 26th may 1966/
2016 LONG LIVE GUYANA

5

He is a Great Devotee

He came from a humble community in Guyana
He later migrates to the United States of America
From there destiny took him to his Mother land India
On his return he was carrying the flag of Hindu Dharma

Wherever he goes large crowd will follow to hear scripter
His melodious voice would charm his listener
He sings to his heart song of devotion
He earns great respect and international recognition

His return to Guyana saw the revival of Hindu Dharma
Large crowd will assemble to hear him at (Function) yajna
This great preacher has won millions of righteous hearts
His lesson was don't get caught in illusion we will have to depart

This messenger and I become close friend while on his mission
His message was honesty, love and devotion
Then one day the supreme God said son time to come home
The great Prakash Gossai was travelling all alone

As he waves goodbye to his followers
His words where you will always be my Sisters and Brothers
Do not leave the path of Religious scripture
Practice love and unity and live together

By Karran P. Deokarran (VICKRAM)
20th March 2016 U.S.A.

A Great Woman

Woman greatness is judge by her action
In life that's her greatest position
Her honesty love and dedication
Help her to win salvation

544 days I spent in a prison cell
My wife Nalenine have a story to tell
Every day she visits the prison gate
With food and water to give she waits

All her hope was my freedom
Sometimes her tears flow at Radom
The enemy tortured she brave
And in court a story she had to give

This woman believe evil cannot survive
She fights to improved others' lives
Wealth and position she never cares
Only the wrath of god she fear

Nalenine become my guiding light
35 years she stood by side and fight
She wants to help free Guyanese from their bondages
As we travel together on this lone voyages

The courage of Nalenine is every women fight
She believes every woman have equal right
Man become the most ungrateful creature
They molest women and then behave like a preacher

It is man solemn duty to protect a woman
To worship her with care and affection
Women is the symbol of man coming on earth
No man has the right to make her hurt

By Karran Deokarran

The Rise Bharat Mata

The people of the great Bharat Mata (India) has finally awaken
The foundation of the Nehru dynasty has been broken
A leader was born to lead the nation to freedom
No more will anyone allowed to hold the Indian at Ransom

From a humble street corner tea seller in Gujrat India
He rises to the world greatest democracy leader
He preaches to his people honesty, love and sincerity
Progress he embraces as his friend and corruption his enemy

His name is Narendra Modi a son of Bharat Mata
At his Mother feet he bows when it was announced he is India next Leader
He looks at the rising sun and bow with a smile
He worshipped Ganga Mata as a poor humble child

This humble son believes in peace and progress
His silence always put the enemy mind to test
His inauguration is one politician will remember
His invitees are those who prepare to work for a bright future

And so the World is about to witness another great change
The once mighty India will move to world highest stage
Fear have already start to linger in many evil minds
Because Modi first act was to seek guidance from the divine

The people of India deserve to regain their pride and glory
And in modi they put their thrust to make history
Time alone can answer all mankind problems in this World
The Indian have proven that the new era is about to unfold

My advice to you Brothers and Sisters of India
You have chosen a leader prepare your future
Your only pride is Bharat Mata [India] history
Your culture, your religion, your unity is your prosperity

175 Years Ago

The sail across the black sea
No one know what their future will be
Today they are a proud family
They maintain a rich culture and living happily

They were fooled to come to Guyana
They were told their work will be to sift sugar
They will be paid plenty of money
Because Guyana is a rich country

This is the British message 175 years ago
In India among the coolie bubo
Then they sail the Indian to a land call Guyana
To work on the sugar plantation, with great exploitation.

The Indian brought with them their culture
They sing and dance while they labor
They British never happy with the Indian life style
The worst of condition was created even for a child.

They Indian believe he that born must die
And that suffering will come to those who lie
Today Guyana Indian has their mark in the world economy
While the British Empire is fading away from history.

By Karran P. Deokarran

A Lone Traveler

A lone traveler I am searching for peace
Everywhere I go the voice of hatred increase
IT fascinating to see how man destroying themselves
Grabbing at illusion which will never help

In Arabia every one pay homage to Allah
In India every one pay homage to lord Rama
In Israel everyone pay homage to Lord Jesus
In America every one saying in God we trust

Every time I try to say of my God
I am disturbed by a missiles going off loud and hard
Every time I try to shout Peace Peace
The news is the death toll increase

God create this world a beautiful place
Oh man your action is a disgrace
You become blind you kill your Brothers and Sisters
Your action is like that of a monster

OH Mother of the ocean   come wash this land
Oh Father of the Air destroy those evil hands
Oh mighty sun burns the evil
Oh creator let peace and love prevail

By Karran P, Deokarran
02/01/ 2016   U.S.A.

The United States of America

They came from every nation to America shore
Because they believe their economic ills can be cure
America is label as the world police man
Everyone feels safe coming to this great American land

America is a safe place to live with a peace of mind
Opportunity to achieve a lifetime reward of any kind
Every country that says America is very bad
Their people are leaving for America happy and glad

For one to know the world come to America
Talk to people from Asia Europe and Africa
Every one story is an experience of bad government
In America they are treated humanely with good intent

Thank you America for accepting people from every nation
They came to you for salvation because of depression
It did not matter who say you are bad oh great America
No one is leaving your shore in search of job in Africa

By Karran P. Deokarran

My Salutation to thee

The American flag I hold in great esteem
The American people I salute who fulfill others dream
You rescue Guyanese from a dictator regime
Your humane behavior everywhere can be seen

Some came legal other illegal you never treat them bad
You give them jobs and comfort to make them glad
You provide their children with education
You give everyone equal protection

Many work hard and make great progress
And help others in their country who live in mess
Those who steal and do wrong things
You ensure their punishment was everlasting

Oh great American to thee I give my salutation
For rescuing my brothers and sisters from oppression
The helping hands you give will be remember
All foreigners will be indebted to your forever

By Karran P. Deokarran

My Salutation Oh God

My salutation to thee oh almighty God on this New Year morning
All through yester year this my only yearning
That whatever had happen in my life yesterday
Will make me stronger to move on in this world today

I look through my window to see the sun shining bright
The same cool wind blowing across the morning light
The whispering of birds can be heard every where
And the sound of Happy New Year fills the air

Then I took a cool bath to refresh myself
Then I go before my alter which is the home of my life
I lite a light to remove all darkness
Then I bow to thee oh God lead me the path to goodness

Oh man you are not this body but a spiritual might
Do not stuff this body with waste it's not right
Your battle is against lust and hatred you must fight
This body to dust it will return prepare your flight

So in 2014 I renew my old vow which I do every year
Action thy duty reward not thy concern my only care
I shall dedicate my life for a better world for mankind
Oh man be honest and loving you will be led into a world of a new kind

I kneel and pray before thee oh supreme creator
Let thy will be done I can only ask for your favor
Grant unto man the will to walk the righteous path
Please do not show them your wrath

History Will Remember Him

He wanted to chartered a new course for a great nation
He wanted to reshape the economy to secure economic salvation
No one understand him he tried several time
He never gives up he is being guided by the divine

He saves this great nation from a third world war
He has the ability to understand a real enemy from far
Peace and love always his priority mission
He was born to lead with a great vision

He sees every one as a friend none his enemy
He is a great fighter guided by his destiny
He always stays awake to watch over evil
He possesses great powers to destroys the devil

On the plaque of history will record his name
Many will have cried who tried to get him defame
He saves a great nation from real poverty
He inherited a nation with a rundown economy

As this great leader embark on his final mission
The wise men start to look at his real position
He will be remembered as a great President of the United State of America
History will remember him as President Barak Hussein Obama

Karran P. Deokarran
Brooklyn N.Y. 1st Jan.2016

Tribute Great Man

In a land of slavery, a son was born
The year was 1918 for Guyana it was a new dawn
A family rejoice a nation hope have risen
Cheddi Bharrat Jagan a name that was chosen

As a little boy he grew with great courage
To send him to the U.S.A. wasn't a disadvantage
His return was like a fire that start to ravage
And Janet by his side ready for his voyage

It wasn't long his mission saw the beginning
And by his side the real fire start sparking
Guyanese joined in their thousands for a great uprising
Everyone knew freedom was coming

The name Cheddi shakes the British crown
Freedom freedom he cried all around
A snake bites him and steals the prize he won
A nation suffers with hatred lust and ruining

A battle for democracy he started
By many intellectual cowards he was assaulted
He breaks the bondage of divide and rule
Peace love and unity was his tools

Jagan call to fight the enemy all must join hand
Many of his colleagues run for safer land
History and time have joined his mission
In 1992 the great beyond made a decision

Those who run return to cheer and clap
And to fit themselves in vacant gap
It wasn't long Cheddi real problem began
Which lead him to the great beyond?

Many years have pass I miss him a lot
Many years I shared his company many things we chat
Cheddi was a man of great honesty
Many he trusted cast a spell on his dignity

The teaching of Cheddi Jagan became renowned
His call for a new global human order was thunderous all around
His vision was to elevate Guyanese sons and daughters
History will revere him as a true Mahatma

By Karran P. Deokarran (VICKRAM)

15

Cheddi Jagan Gone

It was the 6th of March, 1997
A sound came rolling down like thunder
My dear son where are thou
You work hard, you must rest now

Material power is a dream of lust
It comes like the morning sun rise
Listen to everyone cries
And disappear when the sun dust

The dream of democracy will never fulfill
From 1992 to 1997 his heart was hell
His followers have gone astray
Grabbing as if there will never be another day

His belief was a world of unity
For mankind he wanted prosperity
His heart and mind was purity
His mission was to allowed every one equality

He believes action was his duty
Personal reward was never his concern
He spent his life mobilizing and uniting other
He became everyone god father

To say everything will be alright
Was for his followers to continue his fight
Like a coward many become corrupt
And then cried they are taking their worth

His life was a lesson of bravery
He prefers death than slavery
People's welfare was before money
This great son was a teacher too many

As the creator hold his hands
A loud and thunderous cries burst through the land
Those who cause him pain and suffering
Will live long in suffering and fighting

When he came into this world
He had a shapeless mask and a book of rules
Like kings and clown and common people
He was a builder of eternity

As his body pass through Guyana
Many shouted he was our mahatma
In white rob he lay at babu john
While thousand sing Cheddi Jagan has gone

A friend, a teacher
A leader and an admire
I will always
Remember

By Karran P. Deokarran

Happy 95 Birthday

He born in Africa the richest land on earth
A nation that live in poverty which make him hurt
He set his mind on a sacred mission
He embarks on a peaceful revolution

Tortured and imprisonment for him was nourishment
To destroy evil was his only intent
His admirer gives him hope and courage
As he seeks victory on his sacred voyage

To send brave men to prison is to make them wise
It allowed their consciousness to give other's a surprise
History have never said evil has won any fight
India and Africa are lesson for those of might

His 95th birthday is a lesson for all learned men
Bravery dose not lies in a microphone or a pen
Great men are those who face the battle with love
They stand on their feet and face weapon unresolved

Oh great Nelson Mandela my salutation to thee
Like Gandhi your mission was to set poverty free
May your courage and love give you strength to live on?
May your act of bravery be man greatest lesson?

By Karran P. Deokarran

Good Bye Mandela

Like a flower he blossoms in this world
His life and works history will unfold
He departed from his old and weary body
He takes with him the love and admiration of his country

He came into this world like every man
He lives a life of a great human
He lives and work for others
He will be remembered as Africa greatest leader

Great men do not die but leave their body
They live in the heart of Wise men some say it destiny
Nelson Mandela walks the earth with courage and simplicity
Forgiveness, love and reconciliation was his priory

For 27 years he lives in South Africa prison
When he became president he extends an olive branch a great lesson
He always believes the world can only be built on love and unity
His mission was freedom and prosperity

Like Mahatma Gandhi and Martin Luther King
Nelson Mandela was a hero a legendary a great human being
He pierces the heart of his enemy with the sword of love
And with Peace and unity apartheid had to remove

Goodbye Nelson Mandela champion of the poor
Your life style will change the minds of evil for sure
The legacy you left millions will cherish
Go rest in peace, god's blessing and best wish

By Karran P. Deokarran

Man Stupidly

Man build bombs and missiles to destroy earth a home he was given
Then kneel and pray oh Almighty God take me to Heaven
Please forgive me for the wrong I have done
He then walks out of God home and shout I have won

Then God look from above and said with a smile
Go my humble child your bomb will help you in a short while
For whatever you sow you shall surely reap
My promise to mankind I shall surely keep

When man leaves this body he takes no material wealth
Yet while in this body he wants to own the whole world wealth
He steals and kills at the expense of his health
He forgets by God he was sent and by god he will be dealt

Everyday man preforms only sinful action
Every Sunday he prays, to God for his protection
God decided to grant man satisfaction
That is how he created something call confusion

And God said when man will reach the climax of frustration
Then I will send hurricane and tornado to cause destruction
There will be war among every nation
Man has no right to destroy my creation

Oh man your knowledge has fail let only good deeds prevail
Allowed wisdom to lead you on the righteous trail
Stop search the world for material wealth
Search thy conscience for spiritual health

This world will not enjoy peace by any amount of education
But by simple teaching of love and dedication
For man to enjoy goodwill and real happiness
He must awake his self-conscious

By Karran P. D Deokarran

A Humble President

It was 22nd Nov 1963 on the Dallas Street of the U.S.A.
The great America wake up to the call of sympathy
A hero, A state man. A great human had fallen
Only destiny can say why it had to happen.

The bullet that was meant for others
Pierce the heart of the nation most revered Leader
As his body fell to the earth his soul leave with a smile
Great men do not die, killer's think like a child.

50 years later I sit to reflect
On this great American idol with a human intellect
He wanted America to be a great and honorable nation
Somebody feel it was a bad decision.

In this evil age good men do not live long
Evil always want to prove right is wrong.
The world is suffering because of many wrong decisions
One such is John. F. Kennedy assassination.

Gandhi leaves his body by assassin bullet.
The Freedom Fighter Martin Luther fell evil did it?
John. F. Kennedy was sent on the same mission.
50 years later his message is America solution.

By Karran P. Deokarran

A Dream

He had a dream a dream for his People
He wanted fair play and justice for all
His heart pain him whenever he sees discrimination
He then decided to embark on a sacred mission

He preaches of black and white people with red blood
He preaches of unity and loves something everyone should
He wanted a great America for the American People
He believes that with unity nothing is impossible

He embarks on a freedom march to Washington
His enemy have created a plan and took up their position
The assassin's bullet pierces through his loving heart
Another great freedom fighter this body he had to depart

Death can only devour those who have hatred
Martin Luther King JR. was a man of great courage
His departure has brought to the enemy great defeat
His dream has awakened millions on America Street

His death has awakened the world from their long sleep
Freedom Freedom a loud voice cried March on don't weep
Remember me if you wish by loving each other
This will help America and the world to be better

By Karran P. Deokarran

21

Destiny A Great Reward

It was a rare dream I ever had
Then the banging on my door later I became sad
And then a scared seen began
Only to know I was in the enemy hand

Guns and soldiers everywhere
first I thought it was a nightmare
Then a horrible voice I could hear
And suddenly my heart went cold with fear

I was taken out of my bed in the middle of the night
Blind folded I was taken away on a frighten flight
My destination a memory that will be forever
And the memory of the kidnapper torture

While on this scary journey
I ask oh god take care of my family
For I know my mission in this world is over
And this body I will depart through torture

For six days and six night
Many tortures I with stand by god's might
I survive without food and water
By God Grace I live to tell the world later

Electric shocks and beating everyday
To the enemy nothing I have to say
On my knee I walk on rough stone
My head flush in toilet bowl by men unknown

Each night I would sit and pray
Oh almighty God come take me away
For in this world no more I wish to stay
The torture and pain increase every day

As I walk from court to prison
On my shoulder I carry the charge of treason
For 544 days I cried in a prison cell
And await the moment a story I have tell

As a Political prisoner the treatment was rough
My wife always says make your mind tough
The prison food was not fit for scavenger
My wife ensures she take care of my hunger

On a wood floor I lie without cover
Sleepless night among prisoner I am being watch over
The prison library become my best friend
In the devil court I await the hour to stand up and defend

If there is anything to praise will be my wife
She was responsible for giving me a second life
In court like sharp steel she pierces the enemy hearts
And tell the judge and jury the enemies have finished their
part

Where there is no righteousness in the heart
All beauty in the character depart
Corruption and distrust become a reality in Guyana
None have confidence in any political party

My ultimate goal is to see Guyana free
And by God grace every one live in harmony
A united people enjoying peace and prosperity
Then my torture will be my gift to my country

Freedom Freedom

Freedom Freedom loud and hard they cried
Freedom they wanted from the chain to which they were tied
Freedom they wanted from whip that lashes every day
Freedom from the salt to their wound which they receive as pay

They were human why such inhuman treatment
They had their own way of life for which they were sent
No one has the right to slave people for their labor
Nor can there be any forgiveness for such behavior

The African then might have had less intelligence
But the British have proven they had no human sense
They use skill to chain the African for their labor
Today the same African are teachers, Lawyers, and Doctors

The African treatment in Guyana can never be forgotten
The British behavior was inhuman and rotten
The slave master planted hatred in to the African jeans
Then tell the world they are bad this is how they should be seen

I salute the Guyanese African on their freedom anniversary
Let your freedom be a great lesson for every family
Use these moments to build bridges across the ocean of hatred
Let unity and love brighten your future with good deeds

As you reflect on the past you must prepare for the future
Remember your courage and strength was your culture
This was taken away from you during slavery
Now is the time to restore it for your bravery

I urge you my Africans Brothers and Sisters
Let not your past destroy your future
Together we must work to make Guyana a land of Paradise
Shun evil politician it's time to unite and become wise

By Karran P. Deokarran

Mother love

A mother love is like a lotus that never wither
The more care and affection given it become brighter
In this world nothing can replace a mother
Care her, cherish her and love her forever

Those who leave their mother to perish
In search of wealth and fame have nothing to cherish
To become ungrateful to a mother who show you the world
Is like tell god a story that was never told

The gods will never forgive those who neglect their mother
But will ensure that they suffer
For the world to be good and great
Every child must worship their mother with fate

Do not run to church night and day and say I went to pray
And leave your mother home because you afford a servant pay
An ungrateful child has no place in society
A mother love and care is the greatest opportunity

Children if you want god blessing care your mother
God will honor and respect you for ever
Do not allow your mother to live in distress
Your whole life will become a mess

By Karran P. Deokarran

From Logi to Bungalow

My fore parent came from India the land of the great
To Guyana they were brought No one know what will be their faith
On the sugar plantation they had to labor
Living was very rough, but where they came from wasn't better

They came with their culture and their tradition
And a conscience that honesty and truth will remain their religion
The British try every trick to remove from them Hinduism and Islam
They labor in hot sun and rain but maintain their tradition

Some say the Indian were fool with plenty of promises
When they reach Guyana hard labor greet them with surprise
Other say the Indian do not know to read and write
They were given a contract which was a human plight

What ever happened history will remind us it was destiny
The Indian should be thankful the British help them on this sacred journey
The Indian who came should not be remembered as indenture labor
But as Islam and Hinduism greatest messenger

Where in the world today labor in the field is working with suit and tie and in air condition
After 175 years Guyana sugar workers still striking for pay rise and better position
The British give the Indian a country to cherish and own
Many who left behind in India still live in suffering and without a home?

The Indian were given a home which was called Logi
The sing their Koran and Ramayana and live happily
They believe from the sweat of thy brow thou shall eat bread
Their hard work is to remind their off spring not to beg

After five years the Indian were given a chance to return home
They choose to remain in Guyana working on the sugar plantation become a norm
They work hard and save their money for their future happiness
Drinking their daro and smoking their chillum take away all their stress

My salutation to my fore parent who choose to come to Guyana
To the British I say thank you for bringing them out of India
Today there offspring have spread across the world with their religion and culture
They are now some of the world best lawyer, doctor and political leader

Every writers and historian are looking for the torture that was done on the Indian
No one never examine to see what the Indian have brought with them
Torture is happening all over the world every day that has the courage to say
The Indian coming to Guyana will be remember as a historical day

The British give them a Logi to live; they ask God for his guidance
He showers upon them faith and courage as a blessing for their existence
Today their offspring are living in comfort and happiness
The own bungalow, car and plenty of money without any stress

Many writers are still searching for the (kala pani) black water
And what happen in the with by and Hesperus while the Indian were travelers
Today the Indian doing all illegal means to meet the White man country
They leave freedom, living in basement and working in condition of modern slavery

Man have proven today that real slavery endowed in Bachelor, Masters and Degree
The wise man walks with his conscience and slave for people and country
The Logi people had no certificate they had truth, love and honesty
Their hard work become bungalow and will remain for eternity

By Karran P. Deokarran

India Power

There will be another great event in history
This time it will be a British tragedy
Spiritual power sometime remains silent
But reveal itself at the right moment

Very soon there will be trouble in the British crown
Because there is something to India it belongs
The crown will be turning upside down
Until the Koh-I-Noor diamond return to where it belongs

It will not be too late for Britain to ask forgiveness
Rather than to live in distress
India is great for it patient and tolerance
And will accept the koi-in-Noor without vengeance

Our Bible say whatever you so you shall reap
Our Gita remind us of karma man cannot escape
Our Koran tell us the wicked will not escape Allah power
It is better to do the right thing than too sorry at the last
hour

By Karran P. Deokarran

Knowledge and wisdom

The man with knowledge always does talking
While the man with wisdom always keep thinking
Competitive knowledge is destroying the world today
The man of wisdom watches with a smile and walk away.

So what is knowledge and wisdom for man?
And what good or bad it can do for any one
Knowledge is learning everything good and bad
Wisdom is practicing well in the name of god.

The man of knowledge praise himself everyday
He sees himself as a shareholder in the power play
Everything he do the I is more important
Material achievement always his intent

The man of wisdom tries to help others
He sees every human as sisters and brothers
Everything he do the web is more important
To help liberate others is his only intent.

Knowledge was meant for man to search nature
Wisdom is the nectar from knowledge to understand the creator
Knowledge is the opening of the memory door
Enter and discover, have no fear

By Karran P. Deokarran

Kali Yug

Kali Yug the Iron Age is coming to an end
War and terror became every nation friend
There will be no place to call a holy land
The chanting of god name is only a sham

The lust for material wealth become even greater
Truth and honesty have gone with the creator
Lies and deception is the law of every land
Man forget everything is in god hand

When the killing will increase not long from now
Every nation will be fighting over little row
Flood and fire will also take it tool for sure
Two third the world population will no more

Lust passion and hatred will destroy every nation
Peace love and honesty will form the next generation
The final battle will not be long but hard
I bow in reverence to thee the coming of the lord

By Karran P. Deokarran

The Cow

The cow deprives her young it milks, to whom it belongs
She gives me to grow healthy and strong
When I became strong and powerful.
I slaughter her and eat her flesh bellyful.

Am I deserved any sympathy
The cow milk makes me healthy
What a cruel human I became
To kill the cow which replace my mom?

When pain and sickness took my body
I ask why, and complain bitterly
I forget the wrong I have done.
I beg oh god have mercy on your son.

Oh my sister's and brother's
The cow is your second mother
All she need is your love and protection
She nourishes you to fight for your salvation

The cow take care of every humane from birth to death
Those who protect her never live to regret
Worshipped the cow with love and affection
Oh man you will have god protection

By Karran P. Deokarran

A Happy Father's Day

To say I love you dear Father
Is a good way to remember his hard work every day?
But to follow a father foot step
Is the best way to live without regret?

He toils in hot sun a rain daily
Sometimes sleepless night, to make me happy
All he wants to see his children do not go hungry
And that their future will be bright and lovely

My humble salutation to thee dear father
Your love and sacrifice will always be remembered
From a baby you give me care and affection
You hold my hands and teach me the path to salvation

You grow me in a world of trying time
You taught me to look at others with words of divine
You instill in me the courage to help other
I will always remember you a loving father

The bible say honor thy mother and father
This will make your world better
To put them in an elderly home is the worst thing
We surrender to the devil and seek his upbringing

Oh all ye loving children on this earth
Always care your father until he departs
Make him happy and glad each day you live
Even a little mistake you will be forgive

By Karran P. Deokarran

The Price for Sugar

They beat the Dutch and chase them away
This is how the British went to Guyana and stay
The brought people from Africa in chain
Then put them in the sugar plantation to plant cane

From slavery to indenture labor
Many were subjected to severe beating and torture
This is how the British treat human in Guyana
All the slave master wanted is more sugar

When the African start to rebel
They went to India for people many lies they tell
Come to Guyana life will be better
You will live in bungalow plenty of food and sifting sugar

The Indian were loaded in [boat] the Hesperus and with by
In horrible condition to Guyana they journey
Their arrival in port Georgetown was a nightmare
They were treated like animal none to see nor here

Living and working on the estate was horrible
For many living become unbearable
Many for their children to go to school had join other religion
Other hold on to their culture despite more oppression

The African an Indian unite to fight for freedom
The message was to the British you will have to leave and run
We will take Guyana for our labor
No more British Guyana no more slave master.

Democracy

Democracy can never be election to elected a Government
Democracy is to manage the affairs of a country with good intent
Democracy can never be to rule with a majority vote in parliament
Democracy is all about consultation and listening to people comment

Democracy is when leaders can make decision by the street corner
Democracy is when Government can display good behavior
Democracy is all about truth and honesty
Democracy is the highest discipline in any country

Democracy was never for the rich to tell the poor what is right
Democracy was never for the strong to start any fight
Democracy is to see every nation wealth benefit all equally
Democracy is to allowed everyone to live in prosperity

Democracy is fairness and justice which everyone deserved
Democracy is when peace fully every nation problem can be resolved
Democracy is never for Government to portrayed hatred and which hunting
Democracy is when everyone is allowed participating in development planning

Democracy can never be sanction on any country
Democracy can never be for any nation to go hungry
Democracy is to remove government that become dictator
Democracy is when every nation can unite together

Democracy is when government and opposition can discuss development
Democracy allowed one to disagreed to agree with good intent
Democracy must display purity love and honesty
Democracy was design by God for man to display sincerity

By Karran P. Deokarran

My Faith

544 days in a prison cell
Many stories I live to tell
Beating and tortured were many I beg to die
The supreme lord said son don't cry

I was wrong to think the kidnapper was my enemy
The real culprit I dwell in their company
Many have asked why I am leaving
I know what Guyana will be facing

I live six day and night without food and water
All I wanted to defend the PPP for Guyana future
I lied to the Guyanese nation
And was later kick by those in position

Cheddi Jagan was an honest man
The party was highjack by a criminal band
Many have lust for wealth and position
Which lead many good men into a world of corruption

I leave Guyana too, so I can free my mind
And to seek guidance from the divine
To Guyana, one day I will return
For the Guyanese people a new day will born

By Karran P. Deokarran

The Finishing line

Every Human that comes in to this world is on a marathon race
The distance is long and many obstacles one has to face
The sweetness is not found on crossing the finishing line
But rather in relishing all the sight on the way to reach one destination

There is no short cut for any one while on their way
But in this race everyone will have to stay
Even if you take a rest you will have to continue
Everyone must reach the finishing line time is up to you

To come on earth everyone agreed on this race
Lust, greed, hatred, and Passion only slow one Pace
To reach the finishing line quickly
Nourish the mind with Peace love and Purity

My dear Brothers and Sisters the race is yours to the end
Victory is inevitable your moral value you must defend
Time is the most precious thing keep on running
Don't put garbage in to your body your muscle will start hurting

On your way the songs of the bird will make you feel well
The flowers will blossom to give sweet smell
Many animals will be on the way to test your courage
Never turn back, must you complete your voyage?

Everything the eyes can see is to help you on your journey
Do not take them it will only be a burden you will have to carry
Just focus on reaching that magnificent finishing line
Sing the glory of God name you will be there on time

When you start this race you were equipped with everything you need
A shapeless mask, a bag of tools, a book of rules and a sign deed
Follow all the rules carefully as you journey
Used your tools wisely you will assure victory

By Karran P. Deokarran

Marriage

The secret of marriage is to understand each other
Prepare to accept worse or better
Trust and confidence will keep marriage together
And in god name marriage will be forever

God created man and woman for each other in the world
Go forth and build a generation they were told
Trust and cherish each other
Everything will be there to full fill your desire

Greed and lust is the enemy of marriage
Oh man you must choose a safe passage
You came for a special purpose oh man
Remember Marriage is god plan

Oh man do not try to gamble with your life
Don't do the wrong thing and blame your wife
The truth will emerge one day
And a huge price you will have to pay

By Karran P. Deokarran

Good Man Story

Evil became the powerful and motivating
When good men fall asleep dreaming
Wicked men are only allowed to rule
When good men make themselves a fool

Love is the biggest weapon to fight any war
It penetrates the mind and the heart from far
Love destroy ego hatred and lust
It rules over evil with trust

Oh man wake up from your dream
Your love the mightiest weapon ever
Evil have taken over your throne
You will soon be wondering all alone

Oh good men you have a duty to preform
Sleeping and dreaming is not your concern
For a special cause you were born
The world is waiting on you for it reform

By Karran P. Deokarran

Life is a challenge

Isn't it strange that princes, kings, and clowns?
And ordinary human is all renown
Each have accepted their lives in their own way
And whatever each one does he will get his pay

The rich and poor the strong and weak say it destiny
The wise man says it an opportunity
The ordinary man says what wrong have I done
The holy man says I am on my way to god kingdom

Life is to live and live whatever may come
There is nowhere while in this body to run
Whatever the challenge one must accept
When death comes there must be no regret

Man greatest challenge is to accept everything is destiny
Everything one do must be with love and honesty
Whatever happen in this life is what we sow?
Reap them with love despite the difficulty we might know

By Karran P. Deokarran

Peace peace peace

There was nothing like peace among mankind
Nor will there ever be a time of peace of any kind
Every day man makes weapon only to fight
Every human want to prove their might

The fight for economic power is on the rise
Every human one day will have a great surprise
Bombs and guns only display man weakness
Real strength lies in human happiness

Hurricane sandy came and shakes America
Man is killing each other across Africa
The Malaysian airline disappear among great technology
Yet every nation only talks about superiority

The only peace is a peace of mind
To achieve it every human has become blind
Why, lust, greed, and hatred is shining like diamond
Man forget that everything material will despair in the end

Peace everyone is looking in a mirror to see
But it is hidden way down within thee
It is call love thrust and simplicity
It cannot be achieved without truth and unity

Peace peace peace the cry every where
Yet more weapons are created every year
Peace can never be while there is fear
Peace would not come by firing missile in the air

The united nation everyday talk peace
While war and sanction is on the increase
Fear and discrimination is everywhere
Stop making missile then peace will come near

By Karran P. Deokarran

Oh Beautiful Guyana

Guyana a land so sweet and beautiful
With everything for human existence so plentiful
Everywhere are green trees rich soil filled with gold and diamond
And the rain and sun took its turn to nourish its rich ground

As I look through my conscience I start to cry
Everywhere is human frustration why
I search and search everywhere for answers
Then finally I seek refuge at the feet of the creator

Within, a loud voice said there is a limit to everything
For those who think about themselves will achieve nothing
Let love and unity form a human shield
And to the nation of great people the truth will reveal

My advice to leaders of every nation on earth today
Make every one smile before they depart their body
A peace of mind will bring comfort and happiness
Leaders of Guyana you must remove the nation distress

Oh Guyanese one day you will become free
You will have leaders that are dedicated to thee
Modern education always a recipe for confusion
Religious practice, love and unity make the final decision

By Karran P. Deokarran

Religion and Politic

Politics and religion is a one-way road to success
Practice with honesty it will bring happiness
Politic give guidance for economic achievement
Religion guide man to attain spiritual upliftment

God and man are inseparable
As long as man live a life that is honorable
Those who sit and wait for tomorrow
Will only achieve great sorrow

Politic guide everyone to attain material development
Health education and social uplift mint
Leaders are appointed with an obligation
To ensure development take place without discrimination

Religion leads man to go back to god
It teaches what will happen if you do bad
Practice religion for peace comfort and happiness
Religion helps everyone to achieve spiritual success

Guyanese a small population crying for land to produce
Government position to rule and abuse
Every government says we will look into your cry
Until it become easier to get a visa and fly

By Karran P. Deokarran

Guyana Independence

It was 26th May 1966 down came the union jack
In Guyana it will be no more don't ask
Up came the golden arrow head twirling in the wind
A nation with laughter and joy stood close behind

Leader's look on with a divided mind
The birth of a new nation will be of what kind
The fight for freedom was full of hatred and passion
Wise men ask what will tomorrow bring for their nation

The only thing remains from the British oppression
Was the African and Indian culture and tradition
A god given gift for the Guyanese nation
The only path to final liberation

47 years later everyone is asking one question
What have we achieved as a nation?
Hatred, lust, greed, distrust and passion
This we live to treasure as a free nation

Guyana a country with great wealth everywhere
Yet its people living in poverty and fear
Everyone in parliament playing circle tennis game
Fighting for money, power, position and fame

It is sad to say on this Independence Day
The only joy is to live in hope and pray
That one day there will be final liberation
And Guyana will become a free independence nation

By Karran P. Deokarran

Rich Country Poor People

Guyana a land of eighty-three thousand square mile
A nation rich in culture with a hospitable smile
From corriverton in the east to Essequibo in the west
Guyanese are the greatest and the best

Guyana some land rich with bauxite, gold and diamond
Everywhere in its vast land it can be found
Guyana fertile land can produce anything in abundance
Coconut, rice, cane cassava for it inheritance

From the rupunini savannah in the south
To the Atlantic Ocean in the north
Guyanese can master anything in short
They are the brain of Africa and India on earth

Guyanese have master the art of living in poverty
They have survived decade of political disunity
Guyanese were never given a chance to prove their talent
Every Government for themselves with no good intent

For any nation to showcase it ability
The government must be on with integrity
Since Independence every Government fail the nation
All the nation know is suffering and high taxation

Guyanese a small population crying for land to produce
Government position is to rule and abuse
Every government says we will look into your cry
Today it is much easier to get a visa and fly

By Karran P. Deokarran

Guyana a Winner that lost

The British always thought they were mighty and strong
The unity of an ordinary nation shakes the British crown
The rule was very simple united we stand divided we fall
A great lesson by the Guyanese for all

The British wasn't happy that Guyana they will have to leave
Quickly a new idea they conceive
We will give the Guyanese independence
We will sow distrust among the different races as a remembrance

Guyana freedom was a great achievement
Bad political leadership brought only punishment
Fighting among the African and Indian race
Brought to Guyana tremendous disgrace

Distrust is eating every one like cancer
Smart politician looking for political power
Plenty of promises at election to get position
Then all they practice is invincible corruption

Today what independence meant to the Guyanese nation
Robbery, hatred, distrust and corruption
Guyanese it's time to unite once again
Remove evil politician and let honesty rein

By Karran P. Deokarran

A lesson of mankind

Some call it hurricane sandy
Some say it was powerful and windy
Some say it was Mother Nature at work
Some say it is the wind God, why only some get hurt

Whatever had happened and whatever every one say
It was a lesson for everyone to learn in a day
Man must not boast about power
God the almighty can strike at any hour

There are nuclear missiles every where
A small hurricane came, everyone get fear
This is another message God send
Oh ma do good and stop pretend

We must stop hurting each other
Follow the rules of our scripture
Stop boast about who is powerful
Who alive, to their good deeds there should be thankful?

Oh man the time is coming and coming very past
The earth burden not long more it will last
Repent now oh man or thou shall punish
Everything the eyes can see will vanish

Earthquake, Hurricane, Flooding are only warning
These are lesson for man to change their evil thinking
Those who refuse the Almighty warning
Will live to see real material suffering

Karran P. Deokarran U.S.A

Love and Patient

I sit at the door of a mandir to look on
A group of devotes dressing the mandir with love and adoration
I try to search their heart at that moment
Handsome and beauty for the [statue] murti was their only intent

Time and patient was the tool to warp the Devi sari
With love and admiration none get weary
Their necklace and jewelry were all in place
A smile bright as the sun could be seen in all the devotee face

It was amazing to see how the devotees dress their [statue] devata
With a fix mind they wrap their dhoti and kurta
Everyone just admire the looks of their god
Deep in their heart they conclude the job was not bad

Everyone wants the mandir to looks like bhagwan palace
They ensure that all the accessories were on their list
The final touches were magnificent
In the devotee's heart this was their only intent

I then realize why there are mandir and murti
It's an opportunity for man to become great devotees
It helps to build sincerity, love and adoration
Which can help, man on it final destination

It will Happen

Destruction is raising its ugly head
Honesty and love is dead
Corruption will cause the third world war
Deadly missile will fire from near and far

Two powers will be fighting for supremacy
A war will start unknowing
One side will be fighting to protect religion
The other wants to protect its economic position

Millions of people will die
Million loud will be their cry
The earth will be filled with human blood
For righteousness it will be good

This war will be between the east and the west
Everyone will put their weapon to the test
Some will fight in the name of god
Others saying, they want to rid the world of bad

In this war there will be no winner
And there will be no more sinners
A new generation will breed fresh air
They will live happy without any fear

By Karran P. Deokarran

Happy New Year

With folded hands oh God I bow to thee
Let this New Year morning bring happiness to me
Whatever had happened in my life yesterday?
Will make me stronger today

As I look through my window the sun shining bright
And the cool wind blowing through the morning light
The whispering of birds can be heard everywhere
The sound of happy New Year fills the year

I took a cool bath to refresh myself
Then I kneel before my alter the home of my life
I lite a light to remove all darkness
I bow to thee oh God lead me the path of goodness

Oh man you are not this body you are a spiritual might
Do not stuff this body with waste it is not right
Your battle is against lust and hatred you must fight
This body to dust it will return prepare your flight

On this day I renew my old vow which I do every year
Action thy duty reward not thy concern that which I care
I will dedicate my life for a better life for mankind
Oh man be honest and loving you will enjoyed a world of a different kind

Karran P. Deokarran
New Year U.S.A. 2014

A Family of Hate and Fate

Man greatest weakness is failing to try
My story many will ask how and why
A man his wife and kids living happily
Until one day they were about to Part Company

Lust fell into the eyes of the husband
By the time he realizes it was wrong she ties his hand
Then death start too close in and nowhere out
The loving wife stood by his side in tears she shouts

I always cherish and treat him as a loving husband
I pray oh god save him from death hands
Then a god Samaritan came to hear his story
Take him to the house of god and plead for mercy

When mercy was granted joy fill the heart of the wife
The husband begs forgiveness he vow to start a new life
They pledge before god and man to live in unity
And to raise a righteous and loving family

Man must never try to become ungrateful
Especially when they have a wife that is faithful
The lesson can be hard and dangerous
Destruction or death is always a must

Any man who want plenty wife don't marry
It will be a burden you will not able to carry
You will become the laughing stock in history
Your final destination will haunt you in the cemetery

A Workers Prayer

Oh I want to be a good worker
Don't make me work hard oh creator
Let me work with honesty
This will help me preserved my dignity

To work with love I want to cherish
If I labored with hatred I must perish
I don't want to work only to earn a living
But to live and cherish working

I want to reward myself with satisfaction
I want to achieve it through dedication
I want to work hard with my mind and soul
Let this taught in of mind never grew old

I always want to be my own boss
Let this be my guiding light oh creator
If out of action come good and bad
Then to help other; help me oh my god

By Karran P. Deokarran

Guyana

Oh great Guyanese this is your future
First find an honest and dedicated leader
Then set up a government with dedicated worker
Appoint sincerity and truth as your Protector

Forget what happen in the past
Unite the races to break the present impasse
Security must reflect the nation intelligence
With all that happen you have great patient

Oh Guyana put corruption before a firing squad
Use your best weapon, racism must dead
The professional you must look after their head
Ensured politician and get rich do not sleep together in bed

Invoke the present of god the almighty
Preform national religious function annually
Educate your children to walk the righteous path
Or the almighty will look upon u with wrath

You must start your work now in Guyana
Removed all the old political party
Set up the Guyana progressive party
It symbols the sun, it motto toward everlasting unity

By Karran P. Deokarran

Give a Women the White House

When fathers fail children futures
Only mothers can cheer them together
When father's show more concern for strangers
Only a mothers can give children a bright future.

Indira Gandhi ruled India, the world greatest democracy
Margret teacher ruled England once the world conquer.
Bandarnike ruled over Sri Lanka once the evil Rawan kingdom.
Janet Jagan born American rule Guyana with great courage.

Angela Merkel the German chancellor a brave women ruler.
Sheikh Hasina, Bangladesh champion among political leader.
Kamla Bissessar ruled Trinidad the land of the humming bird.
Portia Simpson she leads Jamaica forward.

Cristina Fernandez Argentina president a brave woman.
Benazir Bhutto Pakistan leader a great women fighter.
What are we waiting for oh great American civilization?
Only a mother love will save the nation from destruction.

Oh great American people a women leader is the hope for your future.
A reorganized economy would move on under a women leader.
If we want to tell the world, we are capable to lead you with confident.
We must compete with the world to have a women president.

Foolish men look for flaws to attack his competitor.
Wise men complement other who join in the race for leader.
Poor minds spend all their time attacking each other
Rich mind always advocate to build a bright future

Hillary Clinton wants to brighter American future.
She is a women of motherly love which will make her a great leader.
Her power and authority lie in her affection for other.
Give her a chance she will bring a bright future
BY Karran P. Deokarran (02/10/2016) U.S.A.

My salutation to all Elders

My salutation to thee all our beloved elders
You carried the burden of the past on your shoulder
You have made your mark in history
I promise to continue your legacy

Because you were good mom and dad
We are living happy and glad
You teach us to walk and talk
This is how you make your mark

At this festive season I want to share my joy
When you leave this body you will be happy and glad
You will remember your honest son on earth
And give your blessing to him from above

When you hold my hand to walk and play
You always say that I must take care of you one day
Today I renew that confidence and I pray
Oh almighty god make every elders happy here and on their way

Children must never be ungrateful to elders
There past is history you must always remember
Your elders were responsible for your existence
Always show them love, respect and obedience

Once again my salutation to thee oh beloved elders
You are the symbol of flowers that blossom every day for me
You are the shining light like diamond and ruby
You are the creator, you are history

A Message

Oh all ye little Children sing and dance joyfully
Time is moving fast do what you have to do quickly
There are Guns Bombs and missile everywhere
The maker himself now living in fear

Man believes when he dies he go to hell or heaven
None never return back to say what happen
Every nation now fighting to become the champion
None will be there to hear the finale decision

Oh little children stop listen to what dad have to say
He is making Bombs and missile to kill everyone some day
Spend your last moment loving each other
You will be the chosen ones to be with the Almighty Father

God so love the World he gives man a choice
He said I give you Knowledge live happy and Rejoice
Lust and hatred was shining like diamond
Man rushes for them and become blind

Then God give man a curse so bad
Instead of producing food he produces bombs how sad
Man boost about his great invention
Forgetting he will perish in the explosion

By Karran P. Deokarran

America Hopes

Oh great America why are thou crying
Oh great leader why is you pretending
The great American economy is dying
The great American dream is fading

At one time the sun never set on British isle
And Britain dictates what must happen on the soil
Its powers have cover millions of miles
Today what's left is Britain without a smile

The Russian once claim to be a great nation
And was known as the father of communist foundation
What is left today is a shattered federation
And a nation struggling for its own salvation

Oh America your history is one of bravery
You came out of bloodshed and slavery
It time for your people to live happy
Only then the next generation will enjoy prosperity

Oh great leader cast away the lust for power and position
Look within your borders this is your generation
Forget about war and other nations
Let the legacy of your fore parents be of great admiration

By Karran P. Deokarran

I am an Innocent Child

I am an innocent child came in to this world
Oh mom the earth is so beautiful and bold
The sun, the moon and the star are so lovely
And the whispering of birds flying from tree to tree happily

Oh Dad why I have to wake up by the sound of bombs and guns
Why I have to go to bed hungry when billions are spent on bombs
Is that what my coming in this world would worth?
Is this what Man call peace on earth?

Every morning I woke up I hear quarrelling
Then I hear leaders only talk of sanction and fighting
What would I grow up to be in this world oh Dad?
What would I give to the world everything so sad?

You forsake me for war and wealth
You preach on the pulpit of peace of a green earth
I woke up to see shattered tree and red dirt
Is this what is call peace is this what my life worth

Oh Dad please go to funeral look into the casket
Search for the car bungalow bank account or the missile kit
Please Dad changes your mind and stop war
We will shower praise on you from near and far

Oh children of the world we must tell Dad today
If he does not stop fire guns and missile everyday
Some day we will take the reins of power
Not even his pension will be guaranteed any longer

Happy Birthday

Happy birthday to my grandson
Grandpa wishes you all the best for years too come
Don’t waste all your life on birthday celebration
Be a good son and take good care of your dad and mom

This my gift to you my grandson
Always honor and worshipped your dad and mom
She carries you with love and pain
All she wants is truth and honesty you must maintain

As you grow older every day
Always remember you owed your mom you must pay
Sing praise to the almighty god
That will make her happy and glad

Before you are a bright future
Use every moment in your life to help other
The world will become greater
By history your dad and mom will be remember

By Karran P. Deokarran

Where is Good Teaching

To school I love to go every day
In school I learn to sing, dance and play
In school I learn to say the lord prayer
In school the teacher always says do not litter

Someday I learn to say my alphabet
Some time I learn to count to be perfect
Some time I fight I talk and waste time all-day
The teacher whip will remember me what to do next day

Good morning good afternoon always scarce
To love and understand each other this the wrong place
Peace love and unity cannot be found nowhere
To teaches moral value no one care

When I grow up all I want to be rich
Even to rob my teacher I don't care a bitch
I never grow up with love and care
Math's and English is the message everywhere

Karran Deokarran 23/1 /2016 U.S.A.

Lead me the way

In school all I learn is how to strike
The teacher says their salary never right
The picket line always the topic in school
When we leave school we are the educated fool

To seek material wealth becomes priority
Love and care becomes enemy in a country
No one learn the value of honesty
Religious teaching in school lost in history

Everything we learn everything we achieve in school
The end result we become perfect fool
Diploma and degree create white color crime
This lead to lust and hatred and man finally become blind

A good education starts with strict discipline
Strict moral value creates good teaching
Every student will leave with love and honesty
Which will be good for people and country

Karran Deokarran 23/1/2016 U.S.A.

Good by America

Good by America I am parting your company
Thank you for the safe keeping and the little prosperity
Thank you for your great hospitality
Thank you to allowed me to understand your real identity

The American dream have brought me to your shore
When I woke up it was no more
I traverse from the beautiful Florida to New York
I live in heat and cold a life for me that doesn't worth

When the winter comes it cool and freezing
When the summer comes it hot and burning
I search everywhere for comfort and peace of mind
Work hard and paying bills was the only thing I was remind

I meet people from every country in this world
From different ethnicities and culture many stores I was told
Everyone came because of the American dream
Goodbye I am leaving it no-where to be seen

My experience and advice I wish to share
It is better to die fighting for country and people welfare
Than to follow dreams and go to others land like me
Stress might be the only comfort for thee

By Karran P. Deokarran

Do Not Fight Destiny

Destiny is never about what we want while in this body
It's all about what have to do and we must ready
Five years ago while working to make others' lives happy
To America you and your family must leave immediately

On the plane step I stood and wave Guyana goodbye
It my home, my country, my people I cried
For five hour I sit in the air a million thoughts why
I step out Miami airport touch the soil again I cry

As I settle down a voice came singing
My son not to this place you belong
You will have to move on another journey
Great opportunity awaits you it's your destiny

On the shores of New York, I decided to settle
I found a job to take care of my financial needs a little
A trembling voice revel many stories
With my pen and paper, I reveal great memories

The American dream came smiling before me
A poet and an author a gift from me to thee
Learn as much as you can my child without fear
Your next gift when you become a citizen here

The American flag I shall always honored and respect
Great opportunities lie ahead no one will regret
Thank you oh America for the opportunity I was given
Thank you for giving so many nations a safe haven

Whatever wrong you might have done it destiny at work
Who are we to decided who get help and who get hurt
Everything the eyes can see will vanish nothing will remain
Its happen before it will happen now and it will happen again

By Karran P Deokarran N.Y. U.S.A. 08/23/2016

Don't get caught

There are five places evil dwells
Enter them you become a patron of hell
If one wants to be good and pure
You must keep away from the devil abode for sure

Those who tell lie oh devil they shall be your
Rule over them be their master with great care
Those who visit the home of prostitution
They shall become your loyal companion

Those who consume alcohol they are your company
Make them your servant and friend make them feel happy
Those who visit the gambling table receive them with honor
Oh devil they are your followers be a good master

The fifth and final place I give you oh king of evil
Where ever gold is you shall dwell
Whoever comes to your abode they are your friend
By your dear friend lust they were send

And so this evil age was blessed to rule in five places
Any one enter, Passion, Lust, Hatred, and Anger they will embrace
Oh mankind Stay away from these five places
A good life you will live free from any disgrace

By Karran P. Deokarran

09/01/2016 U.S.A

Wake up Guyana

Wake up Guyanese time is running out
You have a rich legacy why living in doubt
Your fore Parents had a dream
Why only fighting each others can be seen

Every Government come with a good economic policy
Then rule with an iron fist and supremacy
No country can survive without Human development
Guyana greatest failure is to make an attempt

Large building and fancy road is only a show
This will not make the economy grow
Give the poor land to produce food
They will not go hungry but live good

Oh Guyanese when will you become free
Every political leader only their family and friends they see
Unite together if you want a brighter future
Your fore Parents had a dream you must now treasurer

Guyana a great country blesses with wealth
Hardworking people fill with knowledge and health
A nation fills with compassion love and faith
Giving an opportunity they will become great

By Karran P. Deokarran 09/03/2013

Success comes through hard work

He started business from the trunk of a car
He had a vision to go very far
With his wife by his side he journeys into a company
Which lead him to great victory

He employed large number of workers
Many families were able to secure a bright future
His intention
to improve on his business
He is a businessman full of honesty and kindness

His work time start at 3 am in the morning
Working by the side of his workers was good excising
Some worker lazy and will hide away
He would we will find Friday it pays day

With his wife and associate Mr. Barry
Working honestly, they make a name for their family
He is always ready to say to workers good morning
No one can complain he is a bad master but loving and caring

His name is Edd Bero and his wife Rita a hard working family
His associate Barry and his son Coil they all working with great unity
Together with all the worker one can see great improvement in the company
This is the secret that brought to H.L.A. great prosperity

By Karran Deokarran

The Twin Tower came Tumbling Down

As the sun rises from the east to brighten yet another day
The devil and his company decided on a big game to play
It was on the 11th day of September two thousand and one
The battle ground was New York on the twin tower it all began

Like a roaring sound of the thunder the tower came down
The hit was ten second the tower was on the ground
In the heart of the world greatest nation there was no laughter
With sadness and tears three thousand lives have gone forever

The moment has brought great love and unity to help each other
Many were risking their lives to save their sisters and brothers
People did not runaway but run to rescue the helpless
The message was clear for this act you will have great sadness

While every year we remember the love one lost in New York city
We must stay on guard the devil always moves secretly
Let us stay united as a great nation to live happy
Those who want to divide us must not find a place in our company

The lust for personal for pride and power will only make us weak
Leaders who try to divide us must not be giving anything they seek
For us to be a nation united Peaceful, loving and great
We must remember Washington Dream and let it be our fate

By Karran P. Deokarran

MAP OF GUYANA